Waiting is irrelevant

Jane Marjoram

BookLeaf Publishing

Presentation by *BookLeaf Publishing*

Web: www.bookleafpub.com

E-mail: info@bookleafpub.com

ISBN: 9789357214209

First edition 2022

With thanks to my daughter Hannah who gifted me the challenge to write and share this poetry, & to my daughter Imogen & son in law Anthony, who encouraged and teased in equal measure to ensure the task was done!

PREFACE

Poems reveal - but do they reveal all? And do they reveal more about you than me? You are invited to read and discover...

Becoming

Waiting holds back time.
We open our Advent calendars and slowly count
the days.
Mary was 'greatly troubled' and asked
'how can this be?' - nine months of interminable
waiting.

Yet this year's Advent, which begins the
Christmas Wait, was quickly marked
by a goodbye.
She's gone now, the visit might be over,
yet it added to the shape and tenor of
the day.

Four Advent candles: purple for the preparation,
yet third is
rose,
the colour of joy. Rejoice in the moment!
the waiting is
irrelevant.

Advent- arrival - joy at the start then a sad
goodbye; 'Joy and woe are woven fine' (1).
what shapes
our lives is how we change each day.

The evergreen wreath offers hope in the darkness; life is for living now, not waiting for Spring.

(1) William Blake; Auguries of Innocence, 1863

Losing

I know the value of our time altogether
That it is fragile and cannot last.
Each moment doubly precious; with an
uncertain future
But which survived a painful past.

"The important thing is not to have regrets about
your life" I remember saying in my youthful,
ignorant naivety.
Meanwhile the Fates looked down in glee as
regret after regret was being stored up in wait for
me.

the pain ahead of loss is the inevitable
-this I have always known
Time marches on & on but we mark its passing
in celebratory tone.

Each happy time builds my necessary resilience,
ready for that day
When they are gone & I can no longer keep my
dammed up grief at bay.

Choking

It all happened so fast
& then seemed to last
a lifetime.
Exactly a lifetime,
since life was about
to end.

No portents, no hints
that morning: banality was the
pre-show,
preparing for a day
that would not come.
No last words-

speech suddenly impossible;
I gestured helplessly to
my friend;
no shout of panic,
no gasping for breath-
no breath.

The Heimlich Manoeuvre my only
hope; no histrionics - no time
for drama;
as it seemed to fail, a quiet,

inner voice stated ‘you are going
to die’.

Not screamed out, not shouted-
just a numbing acknowledgement.
But not like this,
in front of the kitchen sink,
no preparations, not
ready to die…

At least I would die
in the arms of a friend, yet
so alone
as realisation sank in: aware of
vital minutes from being
no more.

Suddenly the blockage
dislodged & shot out of
my mouth
like a clawing, rasping wild creature,
whilst I had become the
inanimate object.

My emotions were released,
with equal force: the shock, the tears,
the fear,
the coughing and the pain. And relief: I still had
the days ahead,though

forever changed.

Is this how death happens:
just an ending, no fanfare, no time
for regrets;
no last memories of a life lived,
just numb acceptance and a
switch turned off?

No air - gone? Is life that
simple it can be ended on
an instant?
Where's the drama? Where's the loved ones
sitting by the bed, the last words, the
reconciliations, the love?

Choking to death cheats you,
catches you unprepared.
And now?
I remember each second with outlined vividness.
It won't leave me -
waiting is irrelevant.

I feel the arms of my friend
around me; violent,
desperate;
I was not alone: together we
encountered death and forged an
unbreakable bond.

But it remained a banal, foolish,
pointless death, and I live
in fear
of the return of that inner voice:
It’s calm, tone all the more chilling
and compelling.

Swimming

The glint of the water
beckons you
into its sparkling depths and its stillness
invites you
to claim a visible sign of your existence
as you break
its smooth surface. But then you are absorbed
as the water gently engulfs you. You become
diluted
-your individuality diminished-
you are now, simply, sweetly,
a swimmer.
You have entered a swirling painting of ripples
and shimmer; you are that mysterious figure in a
Hockney
pool,
a world apart from any observer (1).
The silk of the water
caresses
your limbs as you slip through the water. The
turquoise
blue tiles below offer a mosaic
canvas
on which you paint as your movements stir

the water - you are both artist and model in an
Ovize's scene (2).
Your body is fabulously
distorted
-submerged and submersed- no need for self
awareness
or consciousness of body image
- you are a Matisse cut out,
a glorious shape
and form - gouache rather than gauche (3).
You have entered a timeless world, where rising
to check the time on the poolside clock is a
curt, abrupt
interruption- a pause when you
surface
momentarily back to the world before gratefully
sliding back into the water's amnesic embrace.
Your watery focus is
all consuming:
the smell of chlorine, the velveteen touch of the
water, the mesmerising sound of your
regular strokes.
You are freed of all constraint, lifted up,
performing
acrobatic feats your clumsy, earthbound self can
only dream of.
The water covers
your anxieties, your 'to do list', your memories,
your plans…

you are softened and soothed.
You swim into the patch of liquid gold where the sunlight
transforms
the surface and it's Midas touch (4) momentarily makes you
glowingly beautiful.
And then Time reels you in. With each step
the weight
of your body returns, the weight of who you are- with each step
the cares
of the world rest upon your shoulders and the your day comes
flooding in.
And yet - does not your body retain a faint memory of that
previous, freeing buoyancy?
And your mind remember that
golden light
and the temporary respite of losing who you really are.

1. David Hockney; portrait of an artist (Pool with two figures), 1972
2. Maude Ovize, Sunday Afternoon, 2021
3. Henry Matisse, The Pool, 1952
4. Ovid, Metamorphoses, Book 11: Midas turned everything he touched into hold.

Walking before breakfast

A year ago- regular walks before breakfast?
Incredulity!
But a lifetime of habits can alter,
instantaneously.
If the shock is sufficient.

It's all in the bones, porous bones,
enlarging the honeycombs.
The silent disease.

Alendronic acid* is no free hallucination
It's possible side effects altered my situation.
Strict conditions:

Take before breakfast, no lying down.
Walking will help so I walk around town.
Sunday early walking.

While neighbours still doze and the birds first
call
I'm surprised to discover I don't mind at all
solitary walking

I walk around the field at the end of my road.
It's now so familiar, in sunshine and cold -

seasons changing.

And I hear in stereo the skylarks' song,
And glimpse the hare, though not for long,
still and silent.

I see the expanse of space around me,
As I walk further and higher I feel truly free,
surrounded by sky.

The fields change from ploughed earth to fresh
new green,
And the wheat turns ripe to a golden gleam,
capturing the sunlight.

Of course, I'ld rather not have it and I'm careful
lest I fall.
Yet I do enjoy my Sunday morning stroll.
Silver lining.

* treatment for osteoporosis

Waiting

A hospital waiting room is a neutral space; the
outcome is uncertain and you don't know what
you will face until you leave
or often some weeks later
when that seemingly innocuous letter arrives, or
worse
a call to speak to your GP and you don't whether
you will survive or whether it was nothing to
worry about.
So you sit in that arid room, keeping your mind
numb
through mindless magazines on so- called
celebrities or a stupid
phone game or setting up a zoom call for later.
Avoiding eye contact with fellow non-travellers
who also don't yet know the way and so all of
you, singularly,
await your fate, unsure of which direction it will
sway- good news or bad.
The stillness is broken, someone calls a name
and for a moment
you recognise a person as their response is
spoken 'I'm here' I exist , no longer a part of the
waiting game.

As they leave, the room settles once more to
Its apathy,
each sitting immobile and detached, quietly
unsure, already anaesthetised in uncomfortable
chairs
until it's their turn to go through the door and
their feelings rush in, their hopes and their fears,
as they prepare to face what's in store
- and the wait is over.

Watching

My cats sit either side of me,
watching
with a steady gaze
as I eat my fish pie,
The path of each forkful from plate to
mouth followed by four eyes until,
self consciously,
I drop a piece and it is clear that's they are
extremely pleased.
Then I spot a hidden paw slowly,
stealthily reaching towards my tray, wanting
more.
My sentinel guards
keeping watch, responsive to every movement
and mood.
I realise I now have a
daily routine
imperceptibility managed
by their desire for pleasure and need for food.
They make you feel privileged that they choose
to be with you.
You find yourself
apologising
if a sneeze or cough disturbs their nap and,
they look at you reproachfully

As they've jump off your lap.
They make it worth the hairball on the carpet,
the daily litter tray chore, as you find yourself
smiling
as your cat gently snores.
They offer their softness,
their purring, being cute, for a life wholly
conditioned
towards their comfort - how astute.
But there's more- as a cat stretches
or curls in full relaxation, if you pause
for a moment
then a cat perspective on the world is an apt
meditation:
let your breathing slow
and doze a while
- just watch and learn
their feline style!

Listening

It was a conscious desire to stop listening-
to music;
an act of self preservation
when feelings could not be allowed
an outlet.
"I don't know how you coped"
They said;
by a surround of a protective silence is the
honest answer.
Silence can be noisy
Leaving no space for grief
or despair
Whereas music is a giant warehouse with high
walls stacked with tagged
boxes of past events
Automatically placed in the conveyer belt
sliding towards you with
no emergency stop button.
You'll discover when it's
time to listen
once more when you find yourself humming a
tune your mind has treacherously selected
behind your back.
And then you are free to bellow a lyric at the top
of your voice and the

bulwark
has been breached
as a
Tsunami of sound
surges in.

Driving

As a child I lay on the back seat —scarce safety
awareness then - staring at the pitch blackness
behind the car
and imagining it would catch up and
devour us.
Now, as I check my mirror, I catch a glimpse of
that
dark entity
and realise that the monster is still there, steady
in pursuit.
The headlights catch
Grotesque shapes
Creating unfamiliar landscapes.
Hedgerows writhe and contort, held back purely
by the
fragile beam.

Beyond the car's small
span of light,
the day's pretty countryside has faded; instead
a nightly drama
for survival as predators seek their prey- there is
no kindness here.
The car radio's
false cheer

emphasises the bleakness outside.
But you cling
to the presenters' voices, listening intently to
things you would normally switch off. Desperate
for
bland human company
to dull your imaginings.
Buildings lurk each side, in shadow, empty and
soulless, stark and y inviting,
offering no comfort.
An occasional lit window
mocks
that you are out there in the wildness of the
night,
alone in the car, a long way still from home.

Dreaming

I'm on a train,
again and again,
The carriage might be
different, but I'm
on the same ride.
The station's ahead and we're
starting to stop
I know I won't make it
to the platform on time.
The reasons may differ, but
the worries remain.
It's a familiar scene;
I've been travelling for years, but never arrive as
I'm far too encumbered however I strive.
So thanks my subconscious for dredging this up,
over and over…
What's up with you?

Transforming

Dispel the fog to look closer:
The hoar frost leaf crisply reveals
its frosty tracery
- one last glorious stand
before it's compost to nurture next year's
growth.
The spider is no longer shunned as we admire
each web
In its icy delicacy;
With its crocheted silver silk; no longer a
trap for the unwary.
The crystalline patterning
on the greenhouse pane glints
like a ballroom of chandeliers- you can almost
hear the waltz.
Each frosted blade distinctly outlined,
crunched underfoot
it demands attention
before next summer it joins the others to be a
lawn to mow.
Each herb frozen,
but offers a hint
of the aroma of warming casseroles to come.
The ice flowers in frozen surprise
at being caught out in this weather;

gone in the thaw but here is
one last sparkling bloom.
And those dismissed as frosty', what of them?
Are they not also
edged with a beautiful fragility?
Maybe that is too much for others to handle and
it is that
lack of compassion
which is more icy than the artic frost. There is
no compensating beauty in such harshness.
Kindness thaws
both the giver and receiver, so what
transformation is here being stalled?
A more bitter cold.

Sitting

Cat on my lap:
such a gentle weight;
a comforting warmth,
I'm encouraged to stay a while.

I follow her gaze
to watch the sparrows
busy foraging in the hedge,
a chorus of communal cheeping,
wings fluttering, buffy brown,
otherwise unseen on a busy day.

Rooks on the roof tops;
oily black blue, roosting sociably.
Gliding elegant red kite,
rusty red brown, forked tail highlighted
against the clouds-
on other days I wouldn't know.

Light casts a shadow
through lead windows;
strange triangles on the wall,
as something solid
melts into a delicate trellis,
then quickly fades- it was a momentary show.

A dog barks in the distance;
skein of geese call as they
co-ordinate their flight;
a faint murmur of conversation,
as goodbyes are given to loved ones, also
travelling,
someone shuts a car door.

The cat stretches;
my reverie is over,
I return to my homely tasks
as she jumps off my lap and onto the floor.

Meeting

Two people
meeting on a screen
create
a complex scene
of intimacy.

Their face appears
in your living room;
chatter
dispels the gloom
you feel.

And you feel you've escaped
as your face appears
smiling
from your worries and fears
for a moment.

Secrets offered
and laughter to share
reveals
that someone does really care
about you.

Meeting over;

goodbyes said
silence
as the screen went dead
you’re left behind.

Sewing

Breathing deeply,
controlling my tremors as the
needle enters and exits
my body,
I'm not numbed, rather full of emotion as it
pierces, in and out.
Thoughts of my own clumsy
darning;
will I look like my old favourite sweater,
similarly patched?
Am I now worn, second hand,
pre-loved,
my value lessened? Though I retain a strong
provenance,
each silver scar tells a story, and that makes a
difference I'm told to
the auction price.
Or am I now embellished, owning an
embroidered tattoo;
my own personalised
number plate?
Personalisation demands an extra cost:
sentimental value.
The silken threads surely mock the
pure silk

embroidery of the flowers laying still
hooped in my sewing basket.
Not so beautiful, some might say ugly,
even if we know that 'beauty is in the
eye of the beholder' but
who will see my scar
and fondly trace it's outline
with their finger tips?
Beauty is 'skin deep' - well my stitches are that
for sure. Love your body is a worthy mantra and
each scar is
part of who we are.
I've been stitched up, but
carry no blame.
I'm free to go. I walk unsteady through the
hospital door
reprieved, sewn up, repaired.
I'm fastened and hopefully won't fall apart as I
return to the world out there. No
lost stitch
to unravel, be undone and leave me in despair.
Am I renewed? Will each stitch add resistance to
face the day? Or damaged, not the one I was,
more wary lest my stitches burst through excess
optimism.

Carving

Does the sculptor
release
what is in the stone; as it
struggles
to come into existence? (1)

Or is the stone's
power
its innocent potential, that
virginal
moment before the chisel strikes?

But the stone rightfully
resists
attempts to impose or
dominate;
it is a symbiotic partnership of

sculptor and sculpture, a story of
creation.
The mallet's transforming
rhythm
echoing the sculptor's pulse;

the embryo grew to the

sound
of the mothers beating
heart
booming in the womb.

Slowly the stone takes a new
identity
and, patiently, over time a
shape
is formed and honed;

over the years personalities are
hewn
by life's experiences,
fashioned
by love, adventure and loss.

The surface is made
smooth,
made free of all
blemish
by sand paper and rasp

Can we be similarly
absolved?
Is the sculptor indeed more
priestly (2)
chiselling away the flaws?

The sculptor is covered in
stone dust;
the excess has been
transferred,
accepting the sins of the world.

Yet what's offered is not
eternal;
stone can chip,smash or
crack;
no guarantee of perfection.

Does the pen then triumph over the
chisel;
the poem outlast the
stone? (3).
But stone endures;

has power even when
broken,
with hints of past
civilisations,
worship and adorations.

As the sculptor
carves
a new form emerges; an
ageless
reflection of their time-bound

identity.

1 Michelangelo's Unfinished Sculptures, Accademia Gallery, Florence
2 Sylvia Plath, The Sculptor: "hands moving more priestlier"
3 William Shakespeare, sonnet number 65

Reading

My good fortune is to have a book before me,
no secret reading necessary; no punishment nor
intimidation.
The words are free to slip off the pages into
my mind
I can face the danger of being taken
unaccompanied
to places far beyond my home and boundaries,
to risk going places out of my or anyone's
control.
I have a safe space to lose myself in the story
and meld with the characters, embracing the
expansion
of my world that can offer.
I have the freedom to open myself to
new possibilities
and explore where that leads.
I can lay aside real time and read until the fading
light
gently returns me to tasks undone, duties
unheeded.
I can allow the words to wriggle into my
sub-conscious
and stay once the book is closed; I will be

changed
by what I've read, from inside out.
A book, once read, is no closed door; I can
re-enter
at any stage, ready to receive the new insights
that are gifted; always there, but
waiting
for me to be ready to receive. What are the
consequences
of such a gateway to freedom? A book is a
dinghy,
a sail boat, a train, a plane, which transports
you away and offers you the chance
to see,
to feel, more clearly. Books challenge
oppression;
patriarchies know a woman who reads is
a threat.

Laughing

I’m hearing distant
peals of laughter; I note the
ringers’ changes
as the jokes unfurl, participating in a
performance of communal
merriment. Are they all aware of the
part they must play?
Peals are not spontaneous
- one false note and the
happy harmony
tumbles
down.

Laughter swells up
amongst friends; emerging from
deep ocean gullies,
a wave of emotion expands, heightened
from a distant storm.
Known sorrow
surely dug the depths which made such lofty
crests - the energy of
grief transferred
into a deluge of
loving
joy.

Laughter lights
up the room; was it therefore
in darkness before?
Like a lightning strike
all are illuminated,
individual shadows dispelled
in a shared
smiling moment.
Its effect lingers; such
seismic activity leaves a
satisfying
after-glow

Breathing

Breathe deeply,
surf the waves,
sigh so the candle gently flutters,
pant in rhythmic circling until
baby takes its first breath.

Struggling to breathe,
the flautist plays through the night to
calm the broken accordion's wheeze.
The urgent puff on the inhaler, or the desperate
parent playing
the breathing game: be the
train, child, that gradually slows and breathes
into the station.

Fill the lungs, then balance
on the edge of the turning tide
until breath expels.
A breathing space to bring
calm; awareness of holistic harmony;
the air breathed has swirled
round the globe -
the world breathes with us.

Words of air (1) expressed in song; the practised
breath releasing the soul;
the notes fly high and true.
Mind and body in unison; lateral breath relaxing
the studied movement
of limbs in graceful pilates and dance.

Shallow breathing now,
an expectant pause,
then breath again;
the long weary vigil
intent on each irregular
life-breath, inhale, exhale,
until the agonal breaths lead to a
final gasp.

(1) Sappho, Athens; Icarus: “Mere air, these words, but delicious to hear.”

Remembering

A madly cavorting snowfall crisply coated
the glacial mountain slopes
(I remember it thus)
at the end of our suburban road.

Time for bed, joyously fearful to hear the
expected shrill jangle
of reindeer bridle out in
that wild, bright night.

A jubilant name calling;
not Santa, but a strangely
expectant Mum & Dad,
flushed with an excitement
that belied their grown up status.

A mysterious, oddly shaped present to be
clumsily unwrapped, childish hands trembling
with anticipation-
the uncertain novelty of not waiting for
Christmas!

A sleek wooden sleigh, perfect in its simplicity-
made for urgent speed;
wondrously we crunched into the glassy night,

three intrepid Artic adventurers.

The exuberant rush as we bravely, breathlessly
dived down the white glistening snow,
fast and furious, the first to mark its pristine
satin smoothness, laughing and carefree.

There is a loneliness in being
the sole memory keeper, but
each snow day I catch a glimpse
of that child wrapped up in her parents'
love in the ice laden air.

Rushing

No time to lose-
can time be mislaid?
Are there hours to be found,
lurking somewhere in the shade?

If we move fast enough,
can we grab them as they flee?
So much catching up to do!
Surely rushing then is key?

But why assume if we're rushing
that we're not taking care?
Careful planning is needed,
of that we're aware

to avoid being swamped,
and stuck in the mire,
we need to keep moving -
go down to the wire

so each second counts,
not by luck but design;
priorities and focus to
keep us in line.

To have a rushed day
brings a satisfied glow
which defies all the gurus
who tell us to slow

down in response
to life in the fast lane,
but since time goes on,
It is quite plain

that in order to keep up
we must still dash about
and enjoy the momentum;
no misgivings or doubt.

When a spa day is scheduled,
temporarily rested,
we collect the bonus
from hours caught and invested.

Recycling

Such waste of time
waiting,
each minute falling in the bin and can't be
recycled.
We can try;
think of vibrant paintings in the gallery at the
bus stop in the rain,
favourite tunes on head phones on the commuter
train,
virtually walk through a garden whilst in the
MRI,
but your mind is not so easily
deceived
taunting with what needs doing in your absence.

There are rooms for waiting; no
recycling
of time offered except magazines
out-of-date;
We can try;
a podcast on your iPad, a story on your phone,
bring your books or knitting, a friend so you're
not alone.
You can do your very best to not comply
with a room designed to

deaden the mind:
sit down, stare vacantly until your turn.

Waiting for my guests to arrive; that strange
pause
between feverish preparations and
welcomed arrival.
All done:
the best glasses out and opened
the wine
the house has been cleaned to make it shine
Nothing left to do but wait for the fun.
In a no man's land
with no time zone in frustrated
stasis,
but I compose this poem
and some precious minutes have been banked.

www.ingramcontent.com/pod-product-compliance
Lightning Source LLC
Chambersburg PA
CBHW051740130826
49812CB00033B/933
9789357214209